HENDERSON COUNTY
PUBLIC LIBRARY
HENDERSONVILLE, N. C.

BICYCLE RACING

by Robert B. Jackson

illustrated with photographs

Henry Z. Walck, Inc. / New York

Acknowledgments

Among the people who helped me in the preparation of this book, M. and Mme. Prosper Abécassis of Vanves, France, and Louis Abécassis of Octeville, France, were most generous in their assistance.

Most of all, however, I am deeply grateful to my wife Marcy who resolutely translated a towering stack of correspondence, newspapers, magazines and tapes approaching Alpine proportions.

All photographs were supplied by Presse Sports of Paris.

COPYRIGHT © 1976 BY ROBERT B. JACKSON

ALL RIGHTS RESERVED, INCLUDING THE RIGHT TO REPRODUCE THIS BOOK, OR PARTS THEREOF, IN ANY FORM, EXCEPT FOR THE INCLUSION OF BRIEF QUOTATIONS IN A REVIEW

Library of Congress Cataloging in Publication Data
Jackson, Robert B.
 Bicycle racing.
 SUMMARY: Traces the history of cycling competitions in the United States and Europe and describes the rules and objectives of various types of bicycle races.
 1. Bicycle racing—Juvenile literature. [1. Bicycle racing] I. Title.
GV1049.J32   796.6   75-12180
ISBN 0-8098-2106-0

MANUFACTURED IN THE UNITED STATES OF AMERICA

Contents

1. *Wheels From the Past,* 5
2. *Round and Round: Track Racing,* 11
3. *"Get a Wheel": Riders of the Road,* 23
4. *Road to the Tour,* 34
5. *The Big Loop,* 48
6. *Tour de France, 1975,* 54

1 / *Wheels From the Past*

MORE AND MORE PEOPLE are whizzing about the United States on bicycles these days. Many cycle as an inexpensive method of short-distance transportation; some ride for exercise; and still others have switched to two wheels in order to save gasoline. Most numerous of all, however, are those who cycle because it is just plain fun.

This cycling boom has been accompanied by greatly increased U.S. interest in the exciting sport of bicycle racing. Growing numbers of cyclists in this country are becoming involved as riders, officials and spectators; many more races are being scheduled; and several new tracks have been built with others in the planning stages.

One result of this expanded racing program has been that U.S. riders are beginning to do much better against the tough international competition. Audrey McElmury of Colorado was the World Women's Road Champion in 1969; in 1973 Sheila Young from Detroit was the first non-Russian World Women's Sprint Champion; the World Junior Sprint Champion of 1974 was Gilbert Hatton of California; and Sue Novara of Flint, Michigan, is the 1975 World Women's Sprint Champion.

Sue Novara of Flint, Michigan, 1975 World Women's Sprint Champion.

While all this cycling activity may seem a new development to many, it is only the partial revival of what was a national craze in the United States before the coming of the automobile. Bicycles and bicycle racing were widely popular here during the 1890's; the first World Cycling Championships were held in Chicago in 1893, and by the early 1900's hundreds of professional riders were competing in the United States—as compared to a mere handful today.

Bicycle racing has been included in the modern Olympics since their beginning in 1896; and our riders more than held their own in the early games. In those days there were also several U.S. World Champion cyclists, among them the first World Amateur Sprint Champion, Arthur A. Zimmerman, in 1893; and Marshall W. Taylor, World Professional Sprint Champion in 1899. Taylor, who was often called the "Black Cyclone" and was the victim of much racial prejudice throughout his career, is usually recognized as this country's first black world's champion.

U.S. cycling competitions were at first similar to those of Europe, short sprint events on tracks and longer races on public roads. Then a distinctively American track event, the six-day endurance race, also became common. In these exhausting meets each rider had to race for six days and six nights continuously, taking only such short rest periods as he dared. The winner of a six-day race in San Francisco in 1899 was able to grind out an agonizing total of more than two thousand miles, but he had to be pulled off his bicycle at the finish; and even after he had been carried to bed, his legs kept pedaling.

This brutal form of racing was eventually banned, with six-day events next being contested by two-man teams, one rider resting while the other raced. Many of these meets were held in the United States during the late twenties and early thirties, but by that time general interest in more conventional forms of bicycle racing—as well as in cycling itself—had nearly vanished.

It was the rapid rise of the automobile that had been primarily responsible for the decline of the bicycle here. Mass production had brought the prices of many models so low that the majority of families could afford a car; and most people in the United States had become automobile-minded. Once the late-blooming fad of six-day competition had passed, bicycle racing was a forgotten sport; and if bicycles were thought of at all, it was only as toys for children.

Meanwhile, just the opposite had been happening in Europe. Cars continued to be very expensive there until well after World War II, so many Europeans kept riding bicycles. Their enthusiasm for bicycle racing grew with each season until it reached such heights that bicycle racing is now regarded as the national sport of several European countries and is second only to soccer in popularity in most others.

The big European races are carried live on television, and they get more press coverage than even the Super Bowl rates here. Top professional riders are bigger celebrities than any of our superstars, and even the most rabid of U.S. sports fans seem listless in comparison to

Bicycle racing is the national sport of many European countries.

some European cycling enthusiasts. Continental bicycle racing is a very big-league sport, indeed; and if our riders are once again to compete against the highly experienced European professionals, they must improve much further still.

2 / *Round and Round: Track Racing*

WHILE IT IS POSSIBLE to race bicycles on flat grass ovals or on cinder tracks, most important track races are held on specially built banked tracks which are much smoother. Outdoor bicycle tracks in the United States, generally surfaced with either asphalt or concrete, range from one-sixth to one-third of a mile around. The majority in Europe are between three hundred and four hundred meters (roughly one-fifth to one-fourth mile) in size, and both ordinarily have gently sloped bankings.

Indoor tracks are usually much shorter and much steeper than the outdoor types. Most often about two hundred meters (just over one-tenth mile) around, their much tighter turns are sharply banked at angles of more than forty-five degrees. Needless to say, a fall while racing inside one of these "teacups" can be very dangerous. Indoor tracks nearly always have the very hard wooden surfaces that permit the highest speeds; and they are frequently portable, being erected temporarily in large halls for particular races.

Indoor or outdoor, the best "velodromes" are the relatively few world-class tracks used for Olympic and World Championship events. They are 333.3 meters (about one-fifth mile) around and have the finest of wooden surfaces. Outdoor tracks are relatively rare in this country, indoor versions are scarcer still, and there are very few world-class tracks in the United States.

Track cyclists race in a counterclockwise direction, and their simplest form of competition is that in which a number of riders start together and race for a set distance. Typically, this is five, ten or twenty miles in this country and twenty kilometers (just under 12.5 miles) abroad. There is also a handicap variation of this type of race in which the entrants leave the start at intervals, slowest first and fastest last.

The several other types of track racing are not quite as simple to understand at first, but they are often of greater interest to experienced fans. Of these, sprinting traditionally has been regarded as the ultimate form, and sprinters have been called the "aristocrats of cycling."

Championship sprinters compete over a distance of one thousand meters (.62 mile), which is exactly three laps around a 333.3-meter track. Until the quarter-finals three riders race at a time in single heats; from then on two riders meet, head-to-head, on a best two-out-of-three basis. There is also a series of consolation-type races called "repêchages" which pit losers against losers after each round. "Rep" winners then get a second chance to advance.

The two contestants in a match sprint draw for inside and outside starting positions before their first race, reverse these positions for the second race, and draw again if a third run is necessary. In each case the outside-starting rider gets a choice of leading or following during the first lap, since the leading cyclist is at a disadvantage under most circumstances.

For one thing, the leader must push against the pressure of the air, while the sheltered follower tucked in behind uses up to twenty per cent less energy. This is similar to "slip-streaming" in automobile racing; and a common tactic of the second sprinter—using conserved energy at the end of the race to "slingshot" out from behind the leader—is typical automobile-racing strategy as well.

The leader also has difficulty watching the second sprinter, able only to peer back over a shoulder or perhaps study a shadow. This can be a drawback because surprise plays a large part in sprinting, the first rider never knowing just when or on which side the second may try to dart past.

One basic tactic of a leader is therefore to stall. The first rider must keep at least a walking pace for the first lap, but after that can try to trick the second rider into taking the lead. This is often done by coming to a complete stop, skilfully balancing the bicycle on the steeply inclined track, moving neither forward nor backward.

If the following rider is good enough, though, he or she may come to a "standstill," too; and a war of nerves can result. During the World Cycling Championships in Montreal in 1974, for instance, two sprinters were balanced on the banking this way, "psyching" each other, for almost eight minutes.

But sooner or later the sudden "jump" finally takes place. Either the leader tries to spurt away or the follower makes an abrupt move to pass—and within a split second both are hurtling around the track. They are timed only during their final two hundred meters, and over that distance top sprinters can average close to forty miles an hour.

Just as important as speed to a sprinter is maneuvering ability. Before the jump the two competitors ride high on the track; at the jump one quickly dives down the

Over the final two hundred meters, top sprinters can average close to forty miles an hour.

banking to pick up more speed and shorten the distance around. An opponent in the lead is likely to counter by sweeping down in front, attempting to "chop" the jumper off; then later may swiftly "hook" upward, trying to squeeze the jumper against the top of the track. A leader who jumps may also employ similar swerving tactics; but once between the two parallel lines circling the lower edge of the track, a rider must stay there. Tricks and tactics are no longer permitted; from then on it is only speed that counts.

Pursuit races, in contrast to sprint events, are flat-out contests of pure speed *all* the way. Two competing riders, or two teams of four riders each, start from exactly opposite positions on the track and try to overtake one another. If one rider or team does catch up, the race is finished, but this seldom happens. Evenly matched competitors will run an entire race and change their relative positions by only a short distance. In such cases the winner is the rider or team first completing the set distance: professional, 5,000 meters; amateurs, 4,000 meters; women, 3,000 meters. (These distances are approximately equal to three miles, two and one-half miles and one and three-quarters miles. Strictly speaking, "professionals" are male professional riders, "amateurs" are male amateurs, and "women" are women amateurs, there being no female professional cyclists as yet.)

In team pursuit the four riders of one team race in a line, front wheel to rear wheel. Each takes a turn at the additional effort of leading, swings high on the track until the others have passed below and then joins smoothly on at the rear. For scoring purposes the time of the third rider is taken at the finish.

Motorpacing is an even more unusual form of competitive cycling, particularly by U.S. standards. During motorpacing each bicyclist is preceded by an assisting motorcyclist who cuts the wind; and this allows the

Team pursuit racing requires smooth riding and much practice to avoid having team members collide with one another.

bicyclist to achieve speeds approaching sixty miles an hour at times. The motorcyclist stands as erect as he can, with the bicyclist following so closely that the motorcycle has to be equipped with a roller-bumper at its rear. During a race each pair has to coordinate its moves exactly, and motorpacing can be very dangerous.

Time trials are a fourth type of track racing, each rider racing individually against the clock for one kilometer (.62137 mile). The contestants start at regular intervals (one minute apart, for example); and after they have all run, the one with the shortest time is the winner.

With no competitor close at hand to give a relative idea of performance, a time trialist must ride to reach total exhaustion precisely at the finish line. Either tiring too soon or saving even a little strength can cost a victory; and time trials are thus known as "the race of truth." In 1975 the World Champion time trialist averaged almost thirty-three miles an hour for the "kilo."

These four types of track racing—sprint, pursuit, motorpaced and time trial—make up the largest part of the annual World Cycling Championships held in a different country each August (although not in the United States since 1912). There are separate World Championship events for amateurs (men), professionals and for women. In addition to the events already described the summer World Championship meet includes road races for all three categories and a one-hundred-kilometer (sixty-two-mile) time trial on the road for amateur teams. A tandem sprint event for amateurs is also run, the last of the big-time races for these once popular two-person bicycles.

The final World Championship event, the cyclo-cross, does not take place until winter; because the more snow and mud there is for this wild race, the better. Cyclocross runs (all men) slog along twisting forest paths, across slippery fields, over logs and through rushing streams on a twenty-five-kilometer (fifteen-and-one-half-mile) cross-country course. Many of the slopes are so steep that contestants have to carry their bicycles up them; and a favorite training exercise of hardy cyclo-crossers is to rush up and down a long flight of stairs ten times a day with a bicycle hanging from one shoulder.

Five of the six Olympic cycling events are also track races: sprint, individual pursuit, team pursuit, individual time trial and team time trial; with the sixth being a road race. Curiously, while there have been many other Olympic events for women since 1912, there are still none in bicycle racing; and all of these races are for male amateurs only.

The U.S. National Championships, conducted annually by the United States Cycling Federation, feature track competition, too. The USCF divides its racers into nine classes: Midget Girls and Midget Boys (8-11); Intermediate Boys and Intermediate Girls (12-14); Junior Women and Junior Men (15-17); Women (18 and over); Seniors (men 18-39); and Veterans (men 40 and over). U.S. National Champions are determined for the Midget through Junior classes by adding points earned in a number of track races.

Other U.S. National Championships are decided for specific kinds of events. Besides road cyclocross and time trial champions for several classes, there are U.S. Women's and U.S. Senior Sprint Champions; U.S. Senior and U.S. Women's Pursuit Champions; U.S. Senior Team Pursuit Champions; and a U.S. Senior Ten-Mile Champion. All these champions can be spotted while racing because of their special red, white and blue jerseys which have a stars-and-stripes design.

Along with championship track racing, exhibition-style track competition has also been popular in Europe, especially as part of the modern six-day events. Six-day racing now takes place only during six evenings—plus a Saturday matinée—and many different types of competition are scheduled throughout that period for maximum spectator interest.

While straight distance races, sprints and motor-paced events are included as well, current six-day meets concentrate on more dramatic fare such as elimination races called "Devil Take the Hindmost." In a "Devil" the last rider across the start-finish line on each lap must drop out, until only a predetermined number of riders are left to fight out a final mass-sprint.

Biggest favorite of all, however, is still the old two-man relay that originated in this country at the turn of the century. Ironically, while these races are barely

A Madison racer slings his teammate into action.

remembered here, they are called "Américaines" in France and "Madisons" (after Madison Square Garden) elsewhere in Europe.

In a Madison one of the two teammates races with the speeding pack while the other slowly circles the track above; then at prearranged intervals they exchange places in a highly spectacular move. The rider who has been resting drops down the banking just as the racing partner approaches; and the racer immediately slings him ahead into the thick of the competition, either by grabbing his hand to throw him forward or by giving a vigorous tug at a special pad in the seat of his pants.

The bicycles used in track racing are shorter than road machines, have stiffer frames and lower handlebars, and also weigh considerably less because they require only a single gear and have no brakes. Overall weight being critical, it is now possible to buy a track bicycle made of super-light materials weighing only eleven pounds. (It costs $1300, though.) As for that lack of brakes, a track racer needs to stop only after the event is over; and he or she does that by rubbing a gloved hand against the front wheel.

3 / "Get a Wheel":
Riders of the Road

THE SEASON for indoor six-day racing in Europe is short, late fall through early winter, but the schedule of road races during the rest of the year is both long and extensive. From February until October there are dozens of bicycle races nearly every week, and crowds of enthusiastic fans line the route of almost every one. During a race all other traffic is barred from the roads being used; but most European car and truck drivers, often cycling fans themselves, seem to accept such inconvenience without question.

There are amateur races, professional races, and races open to both. There are races from place to place, time trials and hillclimbs. There are races along city streets and races through the mountains; races lasting two hours, all-day races, races that run for several days, and even a race that takes three weeks. There are national championship races in June, the World Championship road race in August, and throughout the season a points system is in operation to determine an overall trophy-winner at its end.

European professional bicycle racing is sponsored by large businesses as advertising.

Within this bustling world of European road racing, amateur competition does receive considerable attention both for its own sake and as a "farm system" for the professionals. But the races drawing the best fields, the largest crowds and the most publicity are strictly professional.

Professional bicycle racing in Europe is a highly organized sport that receives heavy financial support from many large companies for advertising purposes. Riders do not compete as individuals but in business-sponsored teams, bicycle and bicycle-parts manufacturers naturally being prominent backers. The range of other products represented has been wide, however, including such varied items as automobile oil, furniture, beer and bathroom tiles.

The riders are primarily Belgian, French, Italian, Spanish, Portuguese and Dutch; but unlike the national teams which preceded these sponsored versions, all members of one team do not necessarily come from the same country. Teams and sponsors vary from year to year, mostly according to economic conditions; and currently most teams have more than one sponsor.

Riders are associated with their teams by the colors of their jerseys. In the 1975 Tour de France, for example, the French team of *Gitane-Campagnolo* (bicycles-bicycle parts) wore red, white and blue striped jerseys; the

Spanish *Kas* (soft drinks) team had blue jerseys with yellow arms; while the jerseys of the Italian *Bianchi-Campagnolo* (bicycles-bicycle parts) team were sky blue with a white stripe.

The name of the sponsor is prominently displayed on these jerseys and also appears in white letters across the bottom of each leg of the riders' black, leather-seated shorts. Then, just in case someone might miss all that, it is again repeated on the visors of the riders' caps. These small white caps, which resemble a house-painter's that has badly shrunk, are often striped to match the riders' jerseys. Further bright touches are added by the cyclists' vivid mitts and also by the varied hues of the bicycles themselves. Thus when a multicolored chain of over one hundred riders winds through the green countryside with the sun glinting off their quietly whirling spokes, it is one of the most striking sights in all of sports.

The brilliant patterns within such a procession shift constantly because riders are continually changing positions as a matter of tactics. It seldom happens that one rider—or one group of riders, for that matter—can lead even a short road race from start to finish. Instead there are usually many tactical moves and countering actions, with the lead changing frequently and much action back in the pack.

Setting up these moves and making correct responses to those of others demands that riders use their heads as well as their legs. Not only do bicycle road racers need the strength, speed and quick coordination of other athletes, plus top physical condition and tremendous stamina; they must also be able to instantly "read" a race and then react immediately.

One factor always to be considered, for instance, is the pressure of the air against the leader. A group of racers will therefore often rotate positions, each rider working up at the front in his turn and then dropping back to "get a wheel," or follow closely in the slipstream of another. By this means the group is able to move at a faster speed than any one member could achieve by himself, so some riders call this "taking the bus."

Another cooperative technique, known as the "fan" is used by riders when they are slowed by a wind. They then form a staggered row across the road pointing into the wind, each rider a bit to one side of the man in front of him. This makes an overlapping shelter in which the unprotected lead is periodically changed as usual.

On the other hand, "breakaways" are highly competitive situations. In these a small number of riders sprint out ahead of the pack, sometimes for considerable distances, to take the lead. Some breaks prove to be the mistake of overeager riders, and others are a move to fatigue possible rivals; but some are a serious attempt to capture first place by "dropping" everyone else behind. A successful competitor will recognize the real "attacks" and go with them, yet not waste effort on unimportant ones.

Once a break has been able to leave the pack behind, the members of that break may or may not "relay" the lead, depending on individual tactics. (Those who do not choose to do so, however, are often called "wheel suckers.") Many breaks are eventually caught and "brought back" by the pack; and it is also possible that a smaller, faster break will split away to drop an original one.

Such basic road-racing moves as these are further complicated by the element of team riding. European road-racing teams consist of one or two big stars surrounded by several riders of lesser ability whom the Belgians call "domestiques," or servants. Not only is a domestique expected to give up his bicycle should his team leader need it as a replacement, he must habitually sacrifice his own chances in the race to those of the star. When the leader is out in front of the pack on a break, his domestiques "defend" him by blocking the pack and slowing it down. Or, if the star is back in the pack, his domestiques will go with a break and try to delay it. And should he be left behind ("off the back" or "out the window") with a puncture, they will relay him to the front.

If domestiques do their jobs correctly, they are likely to be exhausted before the end of a race and finish poorly;

but they will have helped their leader to save his strength and finish well. While stars are paid a great deal and domestiques receive relatively little (teams usually share prize money, though), there never seems to be a lack of domestiques, many of them hoping to someday be the star themselves.

The Sporting Director of the Spanish Kas team advises one of his riders. Note that the rear door of the support car has been removed to allow a quick exit for a mechanic in close quarters.

During a major road race a team's strategy is directed by its combination coach and manager who is called the Sporting Director. He follows the race in a team car which is painted to match the jerseys and bristles with spare bicycles from its roof, pulling up beside his men periodically to give instructions or help. Since there are now riders from more than one country on each team, one Sporting Director has solved the language problem by waving little colored flags as signals.

Each team also has three or four mechanics to work on the bicycles and two or three masseurs to rub down the riders' arms, backs and legs before and after competition. Riders shave their legs to make such massage more efficient and to keep hair out of the many cuts and scrapes they receive.

Another chronic complaint of racing cyclists is saddle sores, the standard remedy for which was once to sit on a raw steak while riding. Weather can be a problem, too, because the race always goes on, sun, fog or heavy downpour. On hot days riders may resort to putting moist cabbage leaves inside their caps, but there is little they can do to ward off the chill when climbing mountains thousands of feet high. And rainy or damp weather anywhere makes colds and other respiratory ailments still one more occupational hazard for road racers.

Whatever the conditions, whatever happens, the racers grind along, competing for well over a hundred miles a day and totaling approximately twenty thousand miles of pedaling each year, including training. They have to eat and drink as they ride, being handed a bottle and a bag of food on the fly as they pass what are called the "feeding stations."

In all of this, road racers not only endure fatigue to the point of prolonged suffering, they also risk serious injury. If one rider in a tightly packed sprint goes down, so can many of those around him; and broken bones are not uncommon in these painful tangles. Even worse is the accident that can result when a cyclist descending a curving mountain road at sixty miles an hour hits a patch of oil or sand. As some degree of protection, European riders wear shock-absorbing "monkey-hats" made of padded leather tubes at times (see photos, pages 17 and 21); whereas in the United States, where protective headgear is always compulsory, riders are beginning to favor plastic helmets.

As one of the most physically demanding of all sports, bicycle road racing has become particularly subject to drug abuse by its participants. In fact, the dangerous practice of taking stimulants to extend endurance became so common that the future of the sport was threatened for a time. Top finishers (plus several riders picked at random) are now tested for drugs at the Anti-Doping Control before standings become official; a positive reaction to the test means suspension and a fine.

Also illegal are such tricks as pushing, jersey-pulling, tripping, Madison-style slinging of a teammate, and reaching over to shift an opponent into the wrong gear. Holding on to the rear of a motor vehicle for a tow while climbing is not allowed either; nevertheless riders do occasionally kid each other about being seen "pushing a car up a hill."

The bicycles used for road racing are light but rugged ten- or twelve-speed machines, weighing under twenty pounds. The handlebars sweep low for the most effective pedaling position and also because a crouching rider offers less resistance to the air. Pedaling efficiency is also increased by straps from the skeletonized "rat-trap" pedals around the rider's shoes, toe clips on the pedals, and cleats in the shoes which slide into the pedals.

The weakest point of a road racing bicycle is its tires. No bigger in cross section than a man's thumb and made of cotton or silk, they weigh seven to ten ounces, carry eighty-five to one hundred pounds of pressure per square inch, and can be easily punctured. However, the wheels turn in quick-release hubs so the rider can stay on and merely lift one end of the bicycle while a mechanic quickly pops in a replacement. After all, no one wants to be called "lanterne rouge" (red lantern), which is the racers' term for last place.

A rapid change of front wheels for Belgian star Eddy Merckx.

4 / *Road to the Tour*

IN JANUARY the professional teams start intensive "spring training" on the French Riviera or in the Italian lake country; then in February the season begins with a series of "criteriums" on the Mediterranean coast. A criterium is a relatively short race of two or three hours in which repeated laps are made around a continuous course of only a mile or two, often on a loop of streets in the heart of a city.

Next the much longer point-to-point stage races begin. Ranging in length from a few days to three weeks, they are contested along public roads through one city or town after another in a series of stages. Each stage is usually considerably more than one hundred miles in length, ordinarily takes the better part of a day to complete, and is a demanding race in itself with its own winner.

After each stage the total elapsed time for all stages to that point is computed for each rider; the competitor with the shortest total time in this General Classification is the overall leader of the race. He often wears a special jersey while he holds that position, each important event having its own particular color. The winner of a stage race is the rider who tops its Final General Classification.

The first big stage race of the year, Paris-Nice, takes place about the middle of each March. This annual "Race to the Sun" covers over eight hundred miles from the French capital down to the famous resort on the southern coast. In 1975 Paris-Nice lasted eight days and consisted of an opening time trial, seven stages on the road and a concluding hillclimb against the clock. The winner, in a total of thirty-four hours, thirty-two minutes and twenty-seven seconds, was a slim, reserved Dutch rider, Joop Zoetemelk of *Gan-Mercier-Hutchinson* (insurance-bicycles-tires), a French team. Zoetemelk had also won Paris-Nice the previous year, but his 1975 victory was of even greater significance. After being badly injured by a fall at top speed in May of 1974, he had to withdraw from racing for the rest of the season, and for a time it had seemed he would not ride again.

Second to Zoetemelk in Paris-Nice of 1975, only a

Joop Zoetemelk winning Paris-Nice in 1975. His support car is behind him, and a television cameraman is shooting from the motorcycle.

minute and thirty-three seconds behind after eight days of competition, was the great Eddy Merckx of Belgium, riding for the Italian team of *Molteni-Campagnolo* (canned meat-bicycle parts). Amateur World Champion in 1964 and a professional since 1965, the dark and impassive Merckx is generally agreed to have been the best rider of the past ten years.

In fact, most experts are convinced that Eddy Merckx is the best of all time. Some riders are fine sprinters, some are excellent time trialists, others are tireless climbers, and still others are fearless descenders; but "King Eddy" has done *everything* superbly, approaching perfection as a rider.

Eddy Merckx of Belgium has completely dominated bicycle road racing for the past ten years.

Courageous and intelligent, competitive to the degree that he is called "The Cannibal," and known for his super-quick recovery from fatigue, he has completely dominated the sport for several seasons. He has earned as much as one million dollars a year from it, too.

Three times a World Champion, Merckx has also won nearly every other major road event at least once for a total of over four hundred and fifty victories. He himself, however, considers his greatest victory to be a track mark he set in 1972, the World One-Hour Record of 49.43 kilometers per hour (30.71 mph).

Still, by 1975 there were signs that the seeming invulnerability of Eddy Merckx might finally be ending. Many thought that the nearly thirty-year-old veteran was not quite as strong in the mountains as formerly, for instance. He had also missed the first part of the 1974 season with pneumonia.

On the basis of the results of Paris-Nice, the press therefore began to suggest that Zoetemelk might at last be the man to beat Merckx in the Tour de France. A twenty-two-stage race lasting three weeks, the Tour de France is the most famous of all bicycle races and the climax of the professional season. So far, Eddie Merckx had not only won the prestigious Tour five times, he had won every year that he had entered.

But the season was just then beginning; and many

important races would have to be run before the Tour began in late June. Three days after the finish of Paris-Nice, for example, Milan-San Remo, the first Classic of spring, was held.

A Classic is a one-day, city-to-city race of great tradition, most of them going back to the early days of competitive cycling. There are now ten or eleven Classics each year, the majority being run before the Tour and the others in the fall. They range in length from one hundred and seventy-five to three hundred and fifty miles and usually count heavily toward the Super Prestige Pernod Trophy. This is awarded at the end of each season as an overall championship by a French liquor maker; and for the past seven years, 1969 through 1975, it has been won by Eddy Merckx.

Milan-San Remo, sometimes called "La Primavera" in Italian after the primroses which blossom about the time it takes place, was first run in 1907. The race now starts from a castle south of Milan, heads southwest to the coast, and then follows the shoreline of the Mediterranean to the little seaside resort of San Remo, just east of Monaco, about one hundred and eighty miles in all.

On March 19, 1975, as the leaders came sweeping down a hill only two miles out of San Remo, Eddy Merckx was still behind. He had won this race five times in the past, but had not been able to enter in 1974 because of his pneumonia. Furthermore, while he did return to form later that season he did not win a single Classic race. Therefore he had been widely quoted as saying he was particularly determined to win Milan-San Remo in 1975.

Now only one mile remained; and pacing the leading trio was Joseph Bruyère, a lieutenant of Merckx. Suddenly another rider left the pack to catch them. Out of the saddle, "on the bottoms" of his handlebars, legs churning for the finish was a twenty-three-year-old Italian, Francesco Moser of the *Filotex* (textiles) team. Member of a well known cycling family and considered a likely star of the future, young Moser made his bid to the accompaniment of loud and spirited cheers from the many Italian fans.

With the finish line drawing quickly closer, a fifth rider, pedaling furiously, streaked into the midst of the four leaders. A master at pacing himself, Merckx was charging at last; and by the time the front-runners hurtled into the shop-lined Via Roma the battle for first place was strictly between Moser and Merckx.

After nearly eight hours of racing, the long contest was decided by this final sprint. Inch by inch Merckx was able to pull ahead of Moser; but the race was still not over, for within the last five hundred feet Moser closed rapidly on Merckx.

Eddy Merckx wins by inches over Francesco Moser, Milan-San Remo, 1975.

Flashing across the freshly painted line on the street, it was Merckx in front by less than the diameter of a wheel. Although cycling winners traditionally raise both arms straight in the air at the finish, this race was so close Merckx had barely enough time to extend his right.

April is an even busier month than March in the heavily scheduled European racing season; and in 1975 there were four Classics on the calendar. Three of them took place in Belgium; and Belgian Eddy Merckx won two of these three, taking a third in the other.

The fourth Classic of April, Paris-Roubaix, is the most famous Classic of them all. Currently the start is made from the lace-center of Chantilly, twenty-five miles north of Paris; and from there the route runs one hundred and seventy miles north to Roubaix, a textile city on the Belgian border. Most of the reputation of Paris-Roubaix, however, is based on its last seventy miles.

Called the "Hell of the North," this part of the race is run over steep and narrow roads that date back to a time when horse-carts were used to haul coal from the local mines. Little more than ruts in some places and paved with large stone blocks in others, they are very treacherous surfaces upon which to race bicycles, especially when combined with the usual spring rain and mud.

During Paris-Roubaix of 1975 the mud was sloppier than ever, thanks to snow just before the race. The "Hell" was so slippery in spots that riders fell again and again, finally having to shoulder their bicycles and trot beside the road like a cyclocross. They were soon completely spattered with mud and it became impossible to tell one from another.

Less than six miles from the finish at the velodrome in Roubaix, while he was in the lead, Eddy Merckx had a flat tire. Punctures are very common in this rugged race, as was the difficulty his support car had trying to reach him on the narrow, jammed road. By the time he had another bicycle, he was behind by more than half a minute.

Thought by some to be out of contention by then, Merckx gradually fought his way back with characteristic determination. Before long he had not only caught the trio at the front, he had out-distanced them. In turn they "brought him back," and all four struggled for the lead over the last few miles, heads low and elbow-to-elbow. As they entered the velodrome for the one and one-half laps that would conclude the race, Merckx was in fourth position. First was tough, strong Roger de Vlaeminck of the Italian *Brooklyn* (chewing gum) team. Like Merckx, de Vlaeminck was a Belgian; and he was the current professional cyclocross champion.

With half a lap to go Merckx pushed back out in front of the speeding group, and the crowd in the velodrome came to its feet. He remained just ahead of de Vlaeminck until they entered the final turn; there he weakened slightly and de Vlacminck dove past on the inside to win by half a wheel. Some fans thought Merckx had mistakenly started his finishing sprint too soon, while others said the extra effort of catching up after the flat had cost Merckx the victory.

Spattered with mud, Roger de Vlaeminck charges through the "Hell of the North," Paris-Roubaix, 1975.

By May emphasis in the professional cycling world shifts from one-day Classics to stage races several days long. The first of the three great national stage races, the "Vuelta de España" (Tour of Spain), begins near the end of April and lasts for twenty days or so with much strenuous climbing in the Pyrenees.

The Vuelta is closely followed by the "Giro d'Italie"

(Tour of Italy). The Giro of 1975 started in Milan on May 17 and finished June 7, 2,423 miles later, with a climb of the snow-walled Stelvio pass between Italy and Switzerland. At 9,049 feet, the Stelvio is the third highest pass in Europe; and team cars were cautioned not to use their horns for fear of starting an avalanche.

The leader of the Giro wears a pink jersey; and at the finish of five previous Giros (including the last three in a row) the pink jersey had been worn by Eddy Merckx. In 1975, however, he had to withdraw from the race at the last minute when he came down with a serious throat infection.

Another disappointment for the Italians in the Giro of 1975 was Francesco Moser's absence. Because Moser's *Filotex* team had decided to concentrate on the Tour de France in 1975, they had sacrificed running the Giro to race in France and Belgium that spring, familiarizing themselves with conditions there in advance.

Moser did return to Italy on the June weekend that national championships are held in several European countries, however. The national winners wear distinctively colored jerseys in competition from then on, and Moser earned the green, white and red of Italy. Upon his return to France he also became the first Italian winner of the Midi Libre, a four-day race in the south in which Joop Zoetemelk placed second.

Roger de Vlaeminck, who had won seven stages of the Giro in 1975 and been its final points-leader as well, won another important June race, the nine-day Tour of

Bernard Thévenet of France, winner of the 1975 Dauphiné.

Switzerland, with Merckx second. And Bernard Thévenet of the *Puegeot-BP-Michelin* (bicycles-gasoline-tires) team won the week-long Dauphiné, named for a region of France, with Moser second and Zoetemelk third.

The curly-haired Thévenet, son of a Burgundy farmer, had been national champion of France and second in the Tour de France in 1973. (In 1974, though, he had been forced to drop out of the Tour with a severe skin disorder.) While Thévenet had been considered a somewhat inconsistent rider in the past, in the Dauphiné of 1975 he outclimbed everyone including Merckx.

As the 1975 Tour de France approached, Moser, de Vlaeminck, Thévenet and Zoetemelk were accordingly regarded as the chief rivals of Eddy Merckx in the great race. Merckx would be attempting to win an unprecedented sixth victory in this Tour. The road would be long and the mountains high; but the many Merckxists all over Europe kept insisting, "Nothing stops Eddy."

5 / *The Big Loop*

THE TOUR DE FRANCE is the biggest annual sporting event in the World in every sense of the word. It contains twenty-two stages, it lasts more than three weeks, and it covers almost 2,500 miles. The route circles the entire country of France, and there is much strenuous climbing in all three of the country's mountainous areas, the Pyrenees, the Alps and the Massif Central. Several *million* spectators turn out to watch each Tour in person, while most of the rest of Europe tunes in faithfully on television and radio. Just to finish the "Big Loop" is a notable achievement for any rider, and the winner instantly becomes a super-celebrity with income to match.

Newspapers naturally devote page after page to the Tour, also; and part of their extensive coverage is the

The annual Tour de France circles the entire country and covers 2,500 miles in three weeks.

series of daily standings needed by fans to keep track of the complex event. Every stage is itself a race within a race and has its own finishing order, first of all. Then, in addition, the General Classification lists the overall elapsed times of the riders for all stages thus far. The leader of the G.C. is the most important man in the race, and he wears a yellow jersey so that he can be quickly recognized.

(This yellow jersey carries the initials "HD" on its shoulders to honor Henri Desgrange, founder of the Tour in 1903. Desgrange selected yellow as the color of the leader's jersey because the newspaper of which he was editor was printed on yellow paper.)

This is just the beginning, because the Tour is also scored under several points systems. The top finishers of each stage are awarded points according to their placings, both the number of points and positions receiving them varying with the type of stage—flat, mountain or time trial. After each stage, points are totaled for all stages to establish the overall points-leader of the Tour; and he wears a green jersey.

Mountain stages are scored separately in still another way. The peaks have been divided into four categories by height and steepness of climb, with points given the first riders reaching their summits according to the degree of difficulty. The largest numbers of points are given for mountains of the first category, down to fewest for fourth. These points, when added together, decide the best climber; and this "King of the Mountains" wears a white jersey with red polka dots.

Next there are the sprinters' "Hot Spots," which are previously selected, highly strategic locations along the route, at least one within each stage. The first five riders to reach a "Hot Spot" get points in diminishing order;

and the total of these points determines an overall "Hot Spot" winner.

Besides all this, teams are scored as well as individuals. Team scoring is also done in two ways, by total elapsed time and by total points, the scores of the three top riders being combined in each case. Members of the team leading on time wear yellow caps and those belonging to the team ahead on points wear green caps.

Each of these awards is sponsored·as advertising by a large business and carries with it a cash prize. Many other presentations are also made, both daily and on an overall basis, ranging from a white jersey for what amounts to "Rookie-of-the-Tour" to awards in such areas as "amiability" and "elegance."

In recent years the Tour has grown so large as to start in another country, the Netherlands in 1973, England in 1974 and Belgium in 1975. Nearly all of its generally circular route winds through as much of the varying terrain of France as possible, however, clockwise one year and counterclockwise the next. Cities and towns along the way change from year to year (many pay large amounts for the publicity-value of being included), but the finish is always in Paris.

Hours before the racers are to come through a specific location, the roads are blocked off and spectators start to assemble. In the country enthusiasts often picnic beside the highway while they wait. More and more people collect, and by the time the competitors arrive at some places their road has been narrowed down to a slender corridor between two great cheering crowds.

Just before the racers pass, the long publicity caravan screams by, horns blaring and public-address systems blasting advertisements. Many of these vehicles are built in the shape of the product they advertise; and from these moving cans, bottles and boxes, samples and promotional souvenirs are thrown to the scrambling fans.

Next come police on roaring motorcycles, many press cars follow, helicopters clatter overhead, and finally the colorful racers themselves can be seen—sometimes in a bunch, sometimes strung out, and sometimes in widely separated groups. They seem strangely silent in contrast to what has preceded them, but fans in the crowd make up some of the difference with applause and shouted slogans—"Go, Eddy!" or "Strength to Moser!" They may also offer drinks and snacks as the riders pass, douse them with cold water on a hot day, or if the road is steep, give a tired competitor a helpful (although illegal) little push.

Once the racers have gone, the lengthy procession is concluded by a second caravan of motor vehicles. These include the team support cars, which are directed by radio from the "command-post" automobile of the race organizers; more journalists, broadcasters and race officials; plus the "sag-wagon" for exhausted riders (which advertises vacuum cleaners) and ambulances.

And if there is a gap between the cyclists and these following automobiles, a few demonstrative fans may pay their ultimate tribute to a favorite rider. Dashing out into the road immediately after he has sped by, they will kiss its surface.

Hot riders appreciate this young fan's cooling spray.

6 / *Tour de France, 1975*

As the first spectators began to congregate beside the roads of France in June of 1975, there was even more for them to talk about than usual. To begin with, Eddy Merckx was seeking his sixth victory in the Tour after all. His original intention had been to race in the Giro instead of the Tour, but he had missed the Italian race because of his throat infection and was competing in the Tour in its place.

Then there had been the bitter exchange of words between Merckx and Joop Zoetemelk during the Tour of Romandy in Switzerland in May. Merckx had allowed a previously little-known rider to win by deliberately "sitting in" instead of attacking, apparently to shame his less aggressive rivals. He later accused Zoetemelk in

particular of not doing his share at the head of the pack and of being only a "wheel-sucker."

As for the other challengers of Merckx, the *Brooklyn* team had not entered the Tour, so Roger de Vlaeminck would not be competing. (This was reported to have been an economic decision, the result of the company's just having to spend a large sum of money to ransom a kidnapped official.) But the Italian fans would be looking for Francesco Moser as he rode his first Tour; and French enthusiasts regarded it as a good omen that Bernard "Nanard" Thévenet would be wearing number 51. This was the same number that Merckx had worn when he won his first Tour in 1969, and also the number of Luis Ocaña when he won the Tour in 1973.

Slight, dark and intense, Luis Ocaña is a Spaniard from southern France who has been a great climber and time trialist when at the top of his form. Unfortunately, he has been troubled by much illness over the years, and he has also taken several bad falls.

His worst was during the Tour of 1971, when he and Eddy Merckx were speeding down the steep Col de Mente in the Pyrenees during a driving rain. Although Ocaña was wearing the yellow jersey, a counter-attacking Merckx was leading the dangerous descent with Ocaña on his wheel. Both were without brakes because of the heavy storm.

A Spaniard from southern France, Luis Ocaña has been a great climber when at the top of his form.

Skidding wildly out of control, Merckx slammed into a rock beside the road and fell; Ocaña crashed behind him. Just then Joop Zoetemelk failed to make the same turn and hit the helpless Ocaña at full speed. Ocaña had to be taken to a hospital by helicopter, and Merckx went on to win the third of his four straight Tours.

Ocaña had to withdraw from the Tour the following year with bronchitis, but returned in 1973 to win. However, just as the victory of Merckx in 1971 had the edge taken from it by Ocaña's accident, Ocaña's winning in 1973 lost importance because Merckx did not compete that year. Ocaña had not ridden very well since then, but he had joined a new team for 1975, *SuperSer* (household utensils) of Spain; and now he hoped to both make a comeback and finally defeat Merckx in a Tour.

Surprisingly, the most popular by far of all the entries in the 1975 Tour had seldom been a winner. Raymond Poulidor, a craggy-featured easygoing Frenchman on the *Gan-Mercier-Hutchinson* team with Joop Zoetemelk, has somehow just missed winning race after race throughout a long career. Often called "Poupou" by his many fans, he has also been known as "The Eternal Second." In twelve previous Tours he had never once won the yellow jersey, although being Poulidor he had come as close as eight-tenths of a second and had also finished second overall three times. Since this might be the last Tour for the affable thirty-nine-year-old veteran, "Vive Poulidor!" signs were waving all along the route.

On the evening of June 26, 1975, fourteen teams

Raymond Poulidor is beloved by thousands of fans in spite of being "The Eternal Second."

composed of ten members each started the sixty-second Tour de France in Charleroi, Belgium. (Being close to home, Eddy Merckx had arrived the day before by bicycle.) The usual Prologue, a time trial, was run there on a difficult 6.25-kilometer (3.9-mile) circuit of twenty-eight turns and two hills, the riders leaving at one-minute intervals.

Winner of the first yellow jersey of 1975, averaging over twenty-six miles an hour, was first-time participant Francesco Moser with Eddy Merckx a scant two seconds behind. Zoetemelk placed sixth, seventeen seconds out; Thévenet was twenty-four seconds behind in eleventh after a fall while warming up; and both Poulidor and Ocaña trailed badly at thirty-four and forty-five seconds, respectively.

On the following day the first road stage of the Tour was contested, with the pack racing northwest to Molenbeek, a suburb of Brussels; then turning southwest to cross into France and finish at the velodrome of Roubaix. This was a total of 202.5 kilometers (about one hundred and twenty-six miles), which the fastest riders covered in a little more than four and one-half hours to average twenty-seven miles an hour, an unusually rapid start for so long a race.

The rookie Moser had kept his slim lead of two seconds over Merckx; and as the Tour rolled quickly along he continued to wear the yellow jersey. Winding from Amiens down to Versailles, city of French kings, the long and colorful procession finished the next stage on the automobile racetrack at Le Mans; then reached the Atlantic coast at the resort of Merlin-Plage, the young Italian still in front.

Here, with 100,000 vacationers jammed along the flat seaside roads, Merckx averaged a blistering 30.5 miles per hour to win the sixteen-kilometer (ten-mile) time trial while Moser placed fourth, thirty-three seconds behind. Merckx took over first place from Moser by thirty-one seconds as a result, and next day he put on the yellow jersey for the eighty-ninth time. Thévenet was then fourth overall (2'7") and Poulidor had moved into a tie for fifth (2'32"). A discouraged Zoetemelk, who had been delayed in one stage by a flat and then suffered from food poisoning during the time trial, was thirteenth (3'8"); and a still struggling Ocaña was twenty-second (3'51").

Heading south and enduring some of the worst summer heat on record, the 1975 Tour pushed on to Angoulême, where Moser came back to win the stage victory. Even so, he failed to gain any time on Merckx there because the two rivals finished very close together in a mass sprint.

From Angoulême to wine-famous Bordeaux, then down to Fleurance they raced, some riders now dropping out from exhaustion and others being eliminated for taking too long. A third time trial was run between

Fleurance and Auch (37.4 kilometers or twenty-three miles); and this proved to be a turning point.

Merckx, back at the peak of his form, won Fleurance-Auch in spite of a flat; but Moser slipped to a seventh-place finish, widening the difference between the two to 1′39″. Thévenet, on the other hand, rode very quickly in the time trial to finish second, only nine seconds behind Merckx, thereby moving up to third in the General Classification (2′20″). Poulidor, sick with a cold, fell to eighth (4′42″); Zoetemelk improved to tenth (4′48″); and Ocaña's sixth spot in the time trial advanced him to twelfth overall (5′14″).

The next day, 917 miles completed, was the first of two "rest days" provided for in the schedule. While most riders cycle even on rest days to keep their training edge, they also get a chance to relax and reflect on how the race is going. At Auch everyone agreed that it was one of the most competitive Tours in years; and with the Pyrenees finally in sight the big question became, "Will Merckx weaken in the mountains?"

In the first of the high stages, Auch to Pau, Merckx was able to maintain his lead; but on the next day, Pau to Saint-Lary-Soulan (perched almost on the Spanish border), the climbing grew more difficult. This stage finished on the summit of a mountain of the first category, and during the final ascent Merckx was passed by both Zoetemelk and Thévenet. They were to finish first and second, with third place going to wiry little Lucien

A fading Merckx about to be passed by Lucien Van Impe on the difficult climb to Saint-Lary-Soulan. Van Impe wears the jersey of the "King of the Mountains."

Van Impe (*Gitane-Campagnolo*) from Belgium. Van Impe, then "King of the Mountains," was also to hold the climbing title throughout the rest of the Tour.

Fourth at Saint-Lary-Soulan was a weary Merckx. While he still kept the yellow jersey, he had given up forty-nine seconds to Thévenet, who was now second overall (1'31"). Zoetemelk's fine stage-winning climb had helped bring him up to third (3'53"), Van Impe was fourth (5'18"), a seemingly revived Ocaña was fifth (6'43"), and Poulidor was seventh (9'56"). Tied for eleventh and almost twelve minutes behind was Francesco Moser, a saddened victim of the Pyrenees.

With the first half of their race behind them the cyclists next turned northeast, passing through Albi in stifling heat to enter the rugged countryside of France's central plateau, the Massif Central. A faltering Poulidor was suffering horribly from bronchitis by this point; and then came startling news that Ocaña could no longer continue because of a very bad saddle sore he had been keeping secret. Once again, perhaps for the last time, his confrontation with Merckx in a Tour had been denied.

Stage fourteen of the 1975 Tour covered one hundred and seven miles from the ninth-century city of Aurillac up to the top of the Puy-de-Dôme, an extinct volcano 4,641 feet high. Attacking as the finish neared, Van Impe broke away; but an alert Thévenet stayed right with him, and they both left Merckx and Zoetemelk behind.

As the leaders toiled up the peak, large crowds on both sides of the road pressed closer and closer to them. Suddenly, about five hundred feet from the finish, a spectator (later arrested) lunged forward and punched Merckx viciously in the ribs. Clutching his side and his bicycle wobbling, he somehow managed to finish third, tied with Zoetemelk, before becoming very ill. Van Impe won the stage and Thévenet was second, Merckx's lead over Thévenet having been cut to fifty-eight seconds.

Merckx had a chance to recover during the second day of rest, at Nice on the southeastern coast where the entire Tour had been flown in an unusual move to begin the next demanding test, the ascent of the Alps. The critical fifteenth stage from Nice up to Pra-Loup, which climbed 1.4 miles high and crossed four mountain passes to finish on the top of a fifth peak, was fought out under a blistering sun.

Merckx plunged boldly down the narrow road descending from the fourth mountain, decisively in the lead, only to abruptly lose his strength on the final climb. He watched helplessly as the Italian veteran Felice Gimondi (*Bianchi-Campagnolo*), winner of the Tour in 1965, pumped by. Then Thévenet passed him to pursue Gimondi, next Zoetemelk left Merckx, and finally Van Impe

Bernard Thévenet won the 1975 Tour de France by defeating Eddy Merckx in the mountains.

dropped him behind as well. Thévenet caught Gimondi to win the stage, and Merckx came in fifth to lose his overall lead of the past nine stages. Thévenet was now the new front-runner by fifty-eight seconds, Zoetemelk was third in the G.C. (4′3″), and Van Impe was fourth (5′14″).

Frenchman Thévenet celebrated Bastille Day on July 14 in the High Alps by not only putting on the yellow jersey but also by winning his second consecutive stage and extending his margin over Merckx to three minutes and twenty seconds. One stage ahead, however, was another time trial; and Merckx was expected to much improve his standing there, time trials being one of his acknowledged specialties.

But as Merckx rode to the start of the intervening stage, he hooked bicycles with another rider and crashed heavily to the ground. Although advised by a doctor and his Sporting Director to leave the race, he said, "It is not my habit to stop." Pressing on, Merckx attacked several times, finished third, and picked up two seconds from a fifth-place Thévenet. That night at the hospital it was learned that he had injured his left hip, knee and shoulder and that his upper jaw was broken.

Undaunted, Merckx kept racing and gained another fifteen seconds in the hilly Morzine-Chatel time trial when he placed third to Thévenet's fourth. (Winning was a surprising Van Impe, already up to third in the G.C.) As the Tour came down from the Alps and rolled through wine and cheese country toward Paris, the courageous Merckx drew more cheers than when he had been wearing yellow.

Just over a mile from the end of the next-to-last stage, Melun to Senlis, he got one final chance. A child ran out of the crowd near the leaders, its mother followed, a chain of collisions resulted, and half a dozen riders went down in front of Thévenet. To avoid hitting them he came to a complete stop; but Merckx wrenched his bicycle around the struggling heap, trying to gain ground.

The strain broke his front fork and he had to finish the stage without any steering, all hope for victory now lost. Nevertheless, Merckx persisted and further reduced Thévenet's overall lead to two minutes and forty-seven seconds. The winner of the stage was a young Belgian, Rik Van Linden (*Bianchi-Campagnolo*), points-leader for most of the Tour and also to be wearer of the green jersey at its finish.

After Senlis eighty-eight cyclists remained of the Tour's original one hundred and forty entries; these survivors had 2,380 miles and forty-one mountains behind them. Now only the final stage remained; and for the first time the Tour de France would be concluded with a criterium in the heart of beautiful Paris.

Nearly a million excited spectators jammed the curbs of such famous streets as the Champs-Elysées and the

Rue de Rivoli that Sunday afternoon, watching the racers against a background of historical landmarks like the Louvre and the Arch of Triumph. Eddy Merckx continued to attack for much of the hundred-mile event; but at the finish both he and Thévenet were well back in the pack, their relative standings unchanged. Thus it was a jubilant Bernard Thévenet, the first French winner of the

For the first time, the Tour de France finished on the streets of Paris in 1975. This is the Champs-Elysées, with the Arch of Triumph in the background.

Tour de France in eight years, who ascended the victory stand to receive his yellow jersey (plus two kisses) from the President of the Republic.

Eddy Merckx finished second overall (2'47"), second in total points and second in the climbing category. Third overall was Lucien Van Impe (5'01"), and Joop Zoetemelk was fourth in the Final G.C. (6'42"). Francesco Moser, an improved climber in the Alps and winner of the white jersey for being the best rookie, placed seventh (24'13"). The valiant Raymond Poulidor came in a distant nineteenth (58'57"), but he and Zoetemelk had helped the *Gans* to win both team awards.

Eddy Merckx certainly did not, as one disappointed loser of the Tour had done in the past, go home and bury his bicycle in the backyard. Instead, the very next night both he and Thévenet began the hectic post-Tour round of criteriums which continues well into August. Although the top finishers of the Tour are paid very good "appearance money" for these short events, they must race as many as two a day at times.

At the end of August the important World Championships, whose winners receive white jerseys with a multicolored "rainbow" stripe, take place; and in 1975 they were held in Belgium. While most fans expected the 165.3-mile professional road race to be another duel between Thévenet and defending World Champion

Merckx, the actual outcome was a great surprise.

Early in the championship, on a slope where the road had been made dangerously narrow by spreading crowds, Merckx fell. Any chance of a personal victory for him before his countrymen was then gone; but Merckx continued to ride hard, willingly acting as a domestique for the benefit of fellow Belgian Roger de Vlaeminck.

Fifteen miles from the finish, however, it was the 1975 Dutch national champion, Hennie Kuiper (eleventh in the Tour), who broke away, held his lead and then won the rainbow jersey. Seventeen seconds behind came a sprinting cluster headed by de Vlaeminck, who did place second. From that same group of upset favorites, Zoetemelk finished fifth overall and Thévenet sixth; while eighth, and attacking to the very last, was Eddy Merckx.

Francesco Moser also fared relatively poorly in the World Championship race, coming in eleventh. During October, however, the young Italian won his first Classic (the Tour of Lombardy in northern Italy, the "Classic of the Falling Leaves"); and that same month a revived Joop Zoetemelk won at Lausanne, Switzerland. Many of the major figures of the historic 1975 Tour de France thus seemed likely contenders in future Tours, and bicycle racing fans everywhere were looking forward eagerly to further exciting competition around the "Big Loop."

J796.6
J
Jackson
Bicycle racing

103323